FRENCH QUILTS MAKING FOR BEGINNERS

The Picture Step by Step Guide on How to Make French Braid Quilts Including French Braid Quilt Patterns and Designs

Boris Joseph
Copyright@2022

1

TABLE OF CONTENT

CHAPTER 1

INTRODUCTION

You have to admire a quilt whose name is derived from a certain haircut. The effect of weaved strands is created by French braid quilts and quilt blocks, which are constructed from fabric strips in patterns or solids, just like the sophisticated 'do. And while they appear to be complicated, they are actually rather simple to put together - even for complete beginners.

Making this quilt may be accomplished in two distinct ways (which is also sometimes called a friendship braid). The first employs a standard ruler, whilst the second makes use of a binding tool that reduces the amount of fabric wasted. Below is a lesson for both approaches, allowing you to pick the one that you prefer the best.

CHAPTER 2

STEP BY STEP TO MAKE FRENCH BRAID QUILTS

Method 1: Using a Standard Ruler

Easy is the difficulty level.

What You'll Require

Fabrics in a variety of hues and patterns are recommended.

Ruler

Cutter using a rotary motion

a mat for cutting

Pins for sewing

As a pro tip, you'll be pressing the quilt block in between each strip, which means there will be a lot of starting and stopping. Instead of constantly transferring fabric on and off the sewing machine, consider chain piecing three or four French braid rows at the same time.

Instructions

1. Prepare your fabric by cutting it.

Cut the cloth into strips that are 212 inches wide. Use precut 212" wide strips to make this process go more quickly.) Cut the strips into pieces that are 7'' long, so that you have six strips of each color.

Tips: If you want a broader block, you may cut your strips to 10'' in length, which will give you four strips of each color in the block.

2. Lay 'Em Out on the Table

Lay down the strips in the manner seen above, alternating them so that no two pieces of the same fabric come into contact. Depending on the height of your quilt, you can use as many strips as you'd want to get the desired effect.

3. Sew a Seam with a Stitch

Flip the tip of the bottom left fabric over to the tip of the bottom right fabric, starting at the bottom of the block. Place the pins in the appropriate places and sew where the strips

cross. After flipping the strips
back to their original positions,
press down the seam toward the
bottom of the block to finish it.

4. Participate in another strip

Select the strip that is right
above the seam that you just
finished sewing. Turn the strip
over so that it is on top of the
ones you just linked. Stitch 1"
from the edge of the strip once

it has been pinned in place. The seam should be pressed toward the bottom of the block.

Continue working your way up to the top of the block, flipping strips down and sewing them together in the same manner as you did in the previous steps.

5. Make a shave

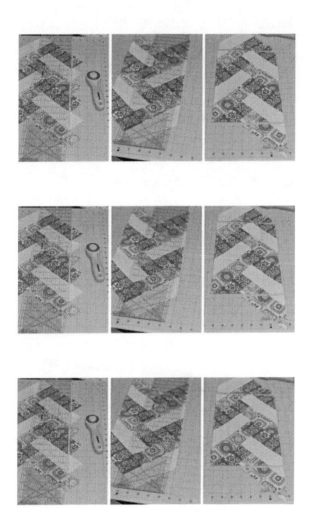

13

Once you've put all of the strips together, align the ruler on the right side of the strip and cut out all of the points to create a straight line. Turn the block over and repeat the process on the other side. To make a rectangle out of the block, square up the top and bottom edges. You've completed your task!

METHOD 2

The Binding Tool is the second method.

Easy is the difficulty level.

What You'll Require

Fabrics in a variety of hues and patterns are recommended.

Tool for tying things together

Cutter using a rotary motion

a mat for cutting

Pins for sewing

Instructions

1. Take Stock of Your Situation

Place a strip of 212" broad
paper in front of you. Align the
straight edge of the binding tool
ruler with one of the short ends
of the fabric strip and cut at an
angle with the fabric strip in

17

place. Rotate the ruler so that the angle of the ruler matches the angle of the fabric and cut once more with it (this time along the straight edge). Cut five of these pieces from a single strip if you have a long enough strip.

2. Arrange the Strips in a pleasing manner.

Lay the fabric strips out in the manner shown in the photo above, alternating them so that no two pieces of the same fabric come into contact with one another. Because the strips are cut at two different angles, you'll have two different looks. It's likely that you'll have to experiment a little to locate a piece that's the appropriate color and facing in the same direction as the others.

3. Sew a Seam with a Stitch

Flip the tip of the bottom left fabric over to the tip of the bottom right fabric, starting at the bottom of the block. Place the pins in the appropriate places and sew where the strips cross. After flipping the strips back to their original positions, press down the seam toward the bottom of the block to finish it.

4. Participate in another strip

Select the strip that is right above the seam that you just finished sewing. Turn the strip over so that it is on top of the ones you just linked. Stitch 1" from the edge of the strip once it has been pinned in place. The seam should be pressed toward the bottom of the block.

Continue working your way up to the top of the block, flipping strips down and sewing them together in the same manner as you did in the previous steps.

5. Make a shave

The top and bottom of the block will only need to be trimmed when it's time to cut after you're finished. After that, you're finished!

CHAPTER 2

HOW TO MAKE A BRAIDED RUG

In this guide, I'll show you how to construct a pretty interesting rug out of your old t-shirts, similar to the one seen. The fact that I used materials I already had on hand meant that this rug didn't cost me any money at all.

Here's everything you'll need to get started:

If you want this rug to be large, you'll need 5-10 old t-shirts for it (I used 5.5 for a small bedside rug)

- a pair of scissors (optional).

- a needle and a length of thread

- sewing machine (optional) (optional)

The longest aspect of this project was the amount of time it took to complete, but the end result was so good that I wouldn't mind building another one in the future. Continue reading to find out how I accomplished this!

Step 1: Make a cut

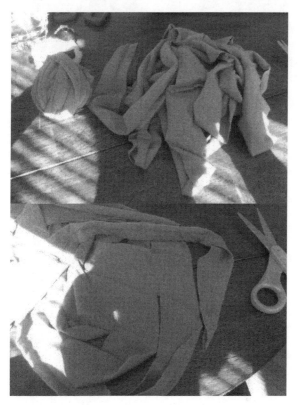

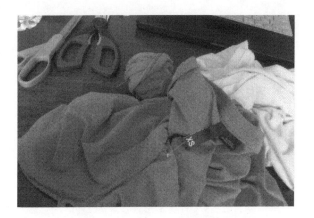

Using old t-shirts from your closet, a thrift store, or your Aunt Marcy's NASCAR t-shirt collection, create a unique look for your little one. The rug I made is around 18" in diameter, and I used 5.5 t-shirts to complete it. However, you might use more t-shirts if you have more time and patience than I do, or if you want a larger rug than mine. It is necessary to prepare the t-shirts for spinning by cutting them into pieces and spinning the pieces into yarn. Rather of following a YouTube tutorial, I photographed each step for inclusion in this article.

In order to do this, you will want to flatten the shirt out in front of you and turn it so that one sleeve points toward you and the other points away from you. Next, take 2 inch measurements every 2 inches from the bottom seam of the shirt (which should be on the left or right side at this point) all the way up to the underside of the shirt's sleeves. Make a mark with chalk or something else that isn't going to be obnoxious-lookingly permanent. Beginning with the first mark or line you drew, you will want to cut along the whole length of the shirt, leaving 3-4 inches of fabric intact on the other side. You may continue doing this until you get to the sleeves, when you should cut all the way through to the opposite side of the seam. As soon as you have cut all of these lines, you may take up the shirt and position it in front of you such that it seems to you to be a ribcage, as seen in the photographs above. See the sliver of cloth on the floor that you left uncut? Now you'll cut it diagonally so that you'll end up with a single long piece of fabric made from your t-shirt instead of two. This is quite difficult to describe, but as previously said, there are a plethora of YouTube videos that demonstrate how to do this, so feel free to browse around if you want more clear guidance.

If all goes according to plan, you should finish up with a rather lengthy strip of fabric from your t-shirt. Stretch this out really, really far and then roll it up into a ball to make it more manageable to carry about. Repeat the process with your remaining shirts.

Braid it in the second step.

Following the preparation of
your t-shirts and the
transformation of those t-shirts
into yarn, it's time to begin
braiding. When I first started

braiding, I used a sewing machine to start the braid and for all of my transitions, but it was only because I was so excited to have received the sewing machine that I "had" to use it. You could absolutely hand-sew all of them together, or you could knot them together for a more carefree appearance.

I started by stitching the end of one yarn strip to the middle of another yarn strip of a different color to form a "T" shape with the yarn. Those were the three sections that formed the beginning of my braid, and when I started braiding, the stitches were covered (which was fantastic!). Continue braiding until you're ready to sew on another color to complete the look. Making a 90-

degree angle between the right side of the cloth and itself, and clipping off the little corner, I was able to add another color to the project. When you stretch it out, the strand will effortlessly transition from one color to the next, creating a beautiful effect. This type of seam is also utilized for quilt binding, as you can see in the image below.

Continue braiding until you have braided in all of your shirts. Finished! If you grow bored of braiding and wish to take a two-week break, you may use an office clip or a chip clip to protect the braid from unraveling. This is what I did. It is beneficial to keep the yarn fully balled up during braiding in order to avoid creating a large, tangly tangle.

Step 3: Make a coil out of it

Prepare your rug by coiling it in advance. Coil it carefully so that it doesn't pucker up into a braided t-shirt bowl (LOL), but be careful not to allow any gaps appear between the rings as you go around the round. While you are sewing, pre coiling this braid will help you keep organized while you are sewing, as well as giving you a sense of the size of your rug and whether or not you will need to add or subtract shirts. When it came to braiding, I was precise (read: OCD) and made sure there was a definite "top" side and "bottom" side during braiding, therefore it's worth adding that I pre coiled with the "bottom" side facing up, because that was what I wanted the stitching to be on.

Step 4: Sew It Together

Begin sewing the ends of your braid together. I started in the centre of the spiral and worked my way around and out of it using a variant of the blanket stitch technique. This is the section that took FOREVER to complete. Seriously. My expectations were high that I would be able to stitch this jerk on the machine, but lo and behold, the dang braid was much too thick to even contemplate fitting under the presser foot. As a result, I manually stitched.

When you arrive to the end of your blanket, weave the ends of your braid into the preceding ring and stitch it to keep it from unraveling further.

Step 5: Put It Down

If you made it through all of those stages, you deserve to sit back and bask in your own awesomeness! Whew.

THE END

Made in United States
Troutdale, OR
05/03/2024

19630252R00022